# STEPHANIE LAMBERT

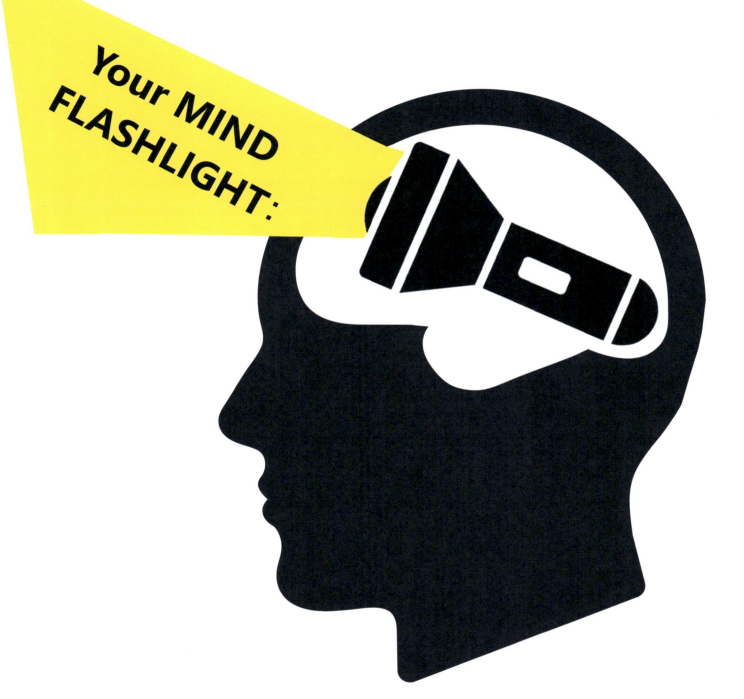

Your MIND
FLASHLIGHT:

# A USER'S GUIDE*

TAKE CONTROL OF YOUR THOUGHTS
TO FEEL THE WAY YOU WANT

*FOR KIDS, TWEENS AND THE ADULTS WHO LOVE THEM

Balboa Press books may be ordered through booksellers or by contacting:

Balboa Press
A Division of Hay House
1663 Liberty Drive
Bloomington, IN 47403
www.balboapress.com
1 (877) 407-4847

Because of the dynamic nature of the Internet, any web addresses or links contained in this book may have changed since publication and may no longer be valid. The views expressed in this work are solely those of the author and do not necessarily reflect the views of the publisher, and the publisher hereby disclaims any responsibility for them.

Any people depicted in stock imagery provided by Getty Images are models, and such images are being used for illustrative purposes only. Certain stock imagery © Getty Images.

ISBN: 978-1-9822-1823-2 (sc)
ISBN: 978-1-9822-1822-5 (e)

Library of Congress Control Number: 2018914779

Print information available on the last page.

Balboa Press rev. date: 01/30/2019

BALBOA
PRESS
A DIVISION OF HAY HOUSE

# Praise for <u>Your Mind Flashlight: A User's Guide</u>*

*"<u>Your Mind Flashlight</u> is a really simple and fun way to empower kids to take control of their emotions instead of their emotions controlling them! The thoughtful approach Stephanie takes to make it relatable helps kids connect with what is being shared. Great book!"* — **Dhaarmika C., – Mom, President and Founder of Camp Kindness Counts**

*"Children struggling with anxiety, stress, depression and other challenges can instantly apply the concept of using their Mind Flashlight to "illuminate" and take back control of their thoughts and feelings. Stephanie's message and step-by-step guide will help readers of all ages feel empowered in their lives!"* — **Amy G., Mom**

*"<u>Your Mind Flashlight</u> is a great book for my boys and I because it was easy for all of us to grasp the content and understand without being too lengthy. My kids and I appreciated the example scenarios, the illustrations and the practice sheets. This book is a great tool for our family."* — **Stacey S., Mom**

*"My 9 year old son and I thoroughly enjoyed reading <u>Your Mind Flashlight</u>. The simple, yet powerful ideas around mindset are so timely for my son at this age, and I am sure we'll continue to reference this book as he gets older. The idea of the thoughts you don't shine your flashlight on disappearing into the dark was very powerful for both of us and I know we'll be chatting about this more as situations arise in daily life. Thank you for such a great book to start some very powerful family conversations!"* — **Alison O., Mom**

*"This book provides a fresh, new tool for understanding interpersonal power – at any age! A kid-friendly read with simple steps to illuminate your child's path to successful social awareness and confidence."* — **Karen R., Mom**

# Foreword

*By: Martha Schlesinger, Ph.D and Licensed Psychologist*

This is a much-needed book. So many of our children feel buffeted by busy schedules, cultural expectations, peer and academic pressures. The frustrating and overwhelming task of trying to succeed in these realms often leads to poor self-esteem and reduced motivation.

Stephanie Lambert has studied this childhood dilemma in her own boys and through a great deal of research and hands on experience. The result is a brilliant, practical guide to help young people find their own power. With the use of their "flashlight" they can let go of the "dark" thoughts of sadness, powerless, poor self-esteem and frustration, and shine the "light" on more positive cognitions. They can learn – in a very creative way – to substitute negative thoughts and feelings for brighter, stronger ideas and beliefs.

The clever illustrations and down-to-earth writing style make this a fun and effortless read. Although this book is intended for young people, I highly recommend it for parents and other adults as well. It provides a creative and effective tool to help our kids (and ourselves as well) become empowered in a complex world.

# Introduction

Being young is pretty great. You are near the starting line of your life when so many things are new and exciting. There are so many possibilities and yearly milestones are the most fun. *Birthdays*? Awesome! *Summer break*? Amazing!

But… sometimes… Do you ever feel like the universe is out to make you feel: **Sad**, **MAD**, **ashamed**, **aWkwArd**, **OVERWHELMED** and overall the exact opposite of anything good?

Do you ever feel like some parts of your life are happening **to you** and you are a helpless victim?

Do you want to keep feeling this way? Would you like to feel differently in those areas of your life?

What if I told you that you can? What if I told you that it's totally do-able to feel: **Confident**, **satisfied**, **at ease**, **positive** and **in control of your life**?

Would you believe me? Would you hear me out?

I hope so, because if you read on *(and this is a short book that even includes pictures. It's not a hard task I promise)*, I'll show you how easy it can be to take command of your thoughts, your feelings and your LIFE.

I wish I had this book when I was younger. I would have enjoyed my kid life a whole lot more.

**It's up to you.**

Use the information from this book to help you understand the power you already have and how to use it to feel what you want, act the way you want and live the life you want.

I wrote this book to help my son *(another kid probably a lot like you)* deal with feelings of helplessness and negativity that he felt at challenging times.

He gave it a shot and found that it works. He *(and I)* hope you will too.


Shine On,

Stephanie Lambert
Redmond, Washington

# Introduction – For Parents, Teachers, Mentors

Please take a moment to quiet the busy world around you… breathe deeply… exhale… then complete this next sentence:

**"If I had a magic wand and could bestow anything onto the young people in my life it would be _____."**

Did you say for him/her/they **TO BE HAPPY**?

I'm not usually a betting woman, but I'd bet dollars to doughnuts you did… along with the majority of the other parents, teachers and mentors reading this introduction.

But here's the harder question. Ready?

**What does it MEAN to BE HAPPY?**

Can I offer a suggested definition? Try this on for size and see if it fits you…

**"Happiness means feeling confident with and accepting myself for who I am *(faults, strengths and everything in between)* and having the ability to take on life's challenges with resilience while being joyfully present to and grateful of all the good that life brings."**

It's a big all encompassing idea of happiness… a "one size fits all" kind of thing.

If that definition of happiness resonates with you and you want that for your kids, this book is kind of like that magic wand we were imagining earlier.

This book can help your child use their brain to empower themselves to feel confident and see the good while dealing with the bad.

It can do the same for you. There is no age limitation.

I developed the **MIND FLASHLIGHT** concept while raising my son. He's a glass half-empty kind of kid. I wanted to give him tools to feel empowered and in control of his thoughts and feelings, especially when the challenges of late elementary and middle school reared their heads.

I wanted to give him some tools he could use to empower himself and in the process, help him to NOT see himself as a victim or feel as one.

This was a tall order due to some anxiety issues and how our developing brains are naturally wired to focus on the negatives and risks in life.

But here's the thing – with this **MIND FLASHLIGHT** tool, he is managing his anxiety and his negative thoughts. He is more positive (*or in some cases, at least more neutral*) and feels more empowered and in control of his thoughts, his feelings and his life. This shift in outlook **changed everything**.

I encourage you to read on and share this with your kid(s). I hope you find it as useful as I and my son do.

Shine on,

*Stephanie Lambert*

Redmond, Washington

*-With love for Hayden & Ronan*

Do you know you have a flashlight in your mind?

**Yep.**

Right there in your brain…

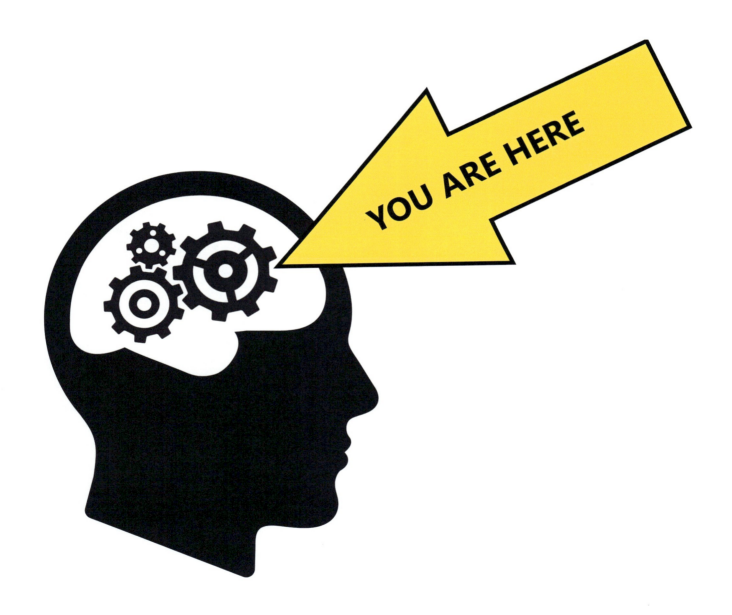

# What is this <mark>MIND FLASHLIGHT</mark> for?

## What is its purpose?

It's there to **illuminate** and **spotlight** the people, places and events of your life.

And just like with your standard battery-powered flashlight –

**YOU** are in control of which direction to shine it.

I'm gonna say it again…
More dramatically this time…

Think of your most

# DRAMATIC & POWERFUL

voice as you read this next sentence…

# YOU

are in

**<u>ULTIMATE CONTROL</u>**

of your **<mark>MIND FLASHLIGHT</mark>**

(*Insert diabolical laugh here*)

MUAH HAHA HAHA AHA!!!

This is pretty darn awesome if you think about it.

Especially because as a young person…

**you may feel like you are NOT in control over much of what happens in your daily life.**

Does this ring a bell….?

# Stuff You Don't Control:

- *When you have to go to school*
- *When you can go to lunch*
- *What you'll be having for dinner*
- *That you have to include your baby brother or sister in just about everything you do*
- *When you have to brush your teeth*
- *When you have to go to bed*
- *When you have to do your homework*
- *When you have to go to practice*

# Even MORE Stuff You Don't Control:

- *What your teacher is going to assign*
- *How easy or challenging those assignments are going to be to you*
- *How your friends are going to behave*
- *What the weather will be*
- *What anyone thinks of you*

# On and on and on....

Seems endless, doesn't it?

So many things you can't control!

At times it can make you feel...

**FRUSTRATED!**

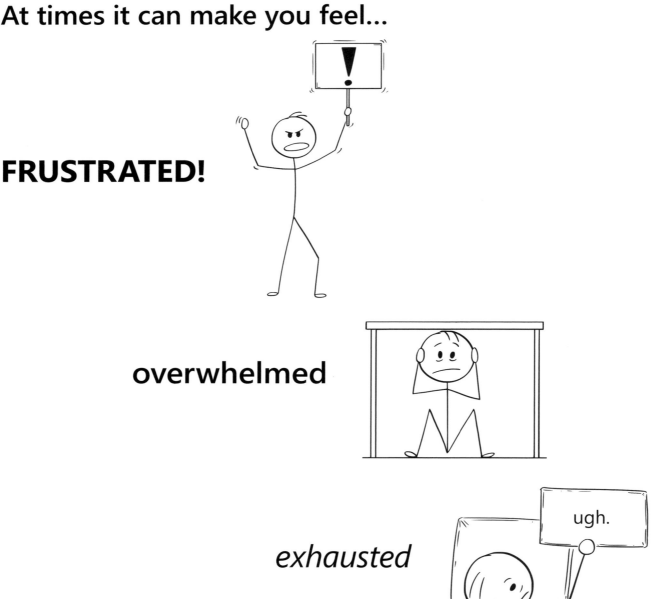

overwhelmed

*exhausted*

and a victim to anything outside of yourself.

# But this...

## YOUR <mark>MIND FLASHLIGHT</mark>?

You have

### COMPLETE

and

### TOTAL CONTROL

my friend.

### And this is VERY. GOOD. NEWS!

Just like with any flashlight – the beam of light it gives off is only so wide.

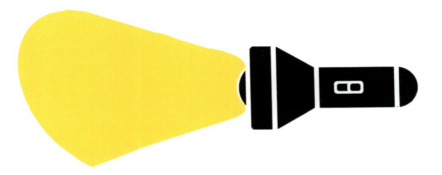

This isn't an overhead light that lights up the entire room.

# Nope.

It will only illuminate and light up a focused area....

...a limited path.

Whatever you choose to shine your
**MIND FLASHLIGHT** on...
that is what ***shapes your thoughts***.

And those **thoughts create how
you'll FEEL** in any situation.

Shine it on the good stuff?
**Think good = feel good**

Shine on the bad stuff?
**Think bad = feel bad.**

Pretty simple when you come right down to it.

The rest of the scene, including:

the people

their actions

the events

taking place that are OUTSIDE of your

==MIND FLASHLIGHT==

beam will be....

You guessed it...

Just like in a dark room where all the nooks and crannies that are not being lit up by a flashlight beam are left IN THE DARK...

**YOUR MIND won't see them**

So...

**YOU WON'T take notice of them either.**

You WON'T take notice

and

You WON'T have a thought about

what is NOT being lit up by
your **MIND FLASHLIGHT**

Those thoughts & feelings WON'T BE

**THOUGHT**                    or                    **FELT**

# If you find you are using your ==MIND FLASHLIGHT==
## to light up things that fill your thoughts and feelings with:

**THOUGHTS:** 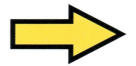 **FEELINGS:**

"That will never work"                          Defeated / Negative

"I can't do that!"                              Self-Doubt

"They are being mean to me"                     Victim / Hopeless

"I'm alone in this"                             Sad / Depressed

"That is totally unfair!"                       Frustrated / Victim

"Everyone is against me!"                       Frustrated / Mad / Victim

"This is too hard!"                             Incapable / Dumb

"I'll never understand this"                    Depressed / Incapable

"I don't have any friends and I never will"     Sad / Lonely / Depressed

REMEMBER – Who has control of your
**MIND FLASHLIGHT**????

That's right...**YOU.**

So, can you –
the one with **ULTIMATE CONTROL** of your
**MIND FLASHLIGHT** -
focus your flashlight beam
SOMEWHERE ELSE?
**YES! YOU CAN!**

# Remember – whatever you DON'T light up with your **MIND FLASHLIGHT** is where?

So that means...

The reverse is also true.

You may be leaving the thoughts you *want* to think... and the feelings you *want* to feel....

**IN. THE. DARK.**

# Ask yourself...

Remember those thoughts we listed before?
Here they are again...

## OLD THOUGHTS:

"That will never work"

"I can't do that!"

"They are being mean to me"

"I'm alone in this"

"THAT IS TOTALLY UNFAIR!"

"Everyone is against me!"

"This is too hard!"

"I'll never understand this"

"I don't have any friends and I never will"

How about using your **MIND FLASHLIGHT**
to shine on some **OTHER NEW THOUGHTS**?

# OTHER ==NEW== THOUGHTS:

**THOUGHTS:**  **FEELINGS:**

"What can I do/change to get it to work?" — Encouraged / Empowered

"I may be able to do that after some work and practice." — Encouraged / Capable

"I can't control how other people act –but I can choose to ignore them and hang out with someone else" — Neutral / Wise

"I bet I'm not the first one to feel this way" — Calm / Compassionate

"I've got friends and family that I can ask for help." — Supported / Cared for

"Is there a reason for me not being able to do this that I haven't considered?" — Thoughtful / Compassionate

"Lots of things are hard on the first try." — Compassionate / Positive

"What can I do to make a new friend today or reconnect with an old friend?" — Excited / Empowered

## *Is it possible?*

# Remember: <u>YOU</u> have <u>ULTIMATE CONTROL</u>

Now that you understand that you have <u>ULTIMATE CONTROL</u> of your <mark>MIND FLASHLIGHT</mark> let's practice using it.

## *Here's the scene:*

You are learning a new and challenging section in math class.

**THOUGHT:**

"I'm never going to be able to do this! It's way too hard!"

**FEELINGS:**

Frustration and self-doubt

# OR…

**THOUGHT:**

"This is challenging, but, I remember feeling like this when I first learned long division and with practice, I got it. I can get this too – with time and practice."

**FEELINGS:**

Capable and Calm

## What feelings do you want to feel?

## Choose the **thought** to

## feel the *feelings*.

It's as easy as that!

Let's try another one...

*Here's the scene:*

Some kids at school call you by
a nickname you can't stand

THOUGHT:

"Man – I can't STAND
that! I've told them
over and over again
that I don't like being
called that and they
just won't STOP!"

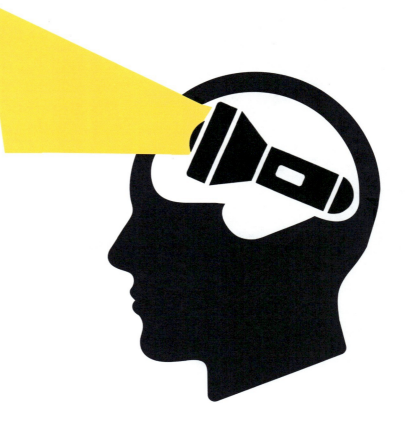

FEELINGS:

Helpless, out of control,
victimized, frustrated

# OR…

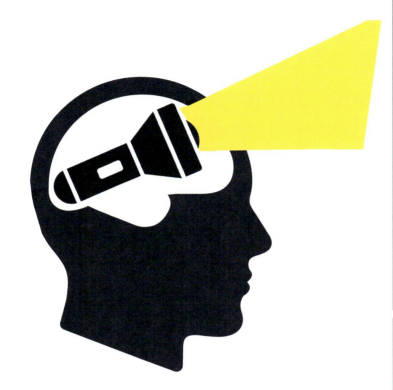

**THOUGHT:**

"I'm going to turn my attention to my other friends, or make a new friend.  I can't control how anyone else acts but I can control how I act."

(this leaves those other bummer thoughts and feelings IN. THE. DARK.)

**FEELINGS:**

Empowered, strong, capable, in control

## So… What feelings do you want to feel?

*Remember…*

## YOU ARE IN CONTROL

## of your thoughts and feelings.

# How about this one....

## *Here's the scene:*

You are feeling stressed out trying to finish homework after a long day of school, baseball practice and a piano lesson.

**THOUGHT:**

"I'm never going to finish this! The amount of work is unfair! This teacher is out to get me!"

**FEELINGS:**

Stressed, Frustrated, Helpless

# OR...

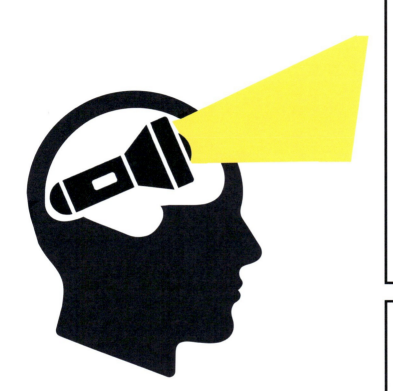

**THOUGHT:**

"I've got a lot on my plate. This is a lot for anyone. I'm going to talk to my parents to let them know that I need help in figuring out a schedule that will work better for me. Maybe I can talk to the teacher as well."

**FEELINGS:**

Hopeful, Empowered, Calm

You don't have to feel like your life is happening to you and you don't have any say....

## *The trick?*

Take a breath, slow down and ***ask your brain to help you*** come up with a thought that will help you feel the way you want to feel.

**OK.** Now it's **YOUR** turn. Think about some things that are upsetting you or challenging you right now in your life. Plug it into the boxes below...

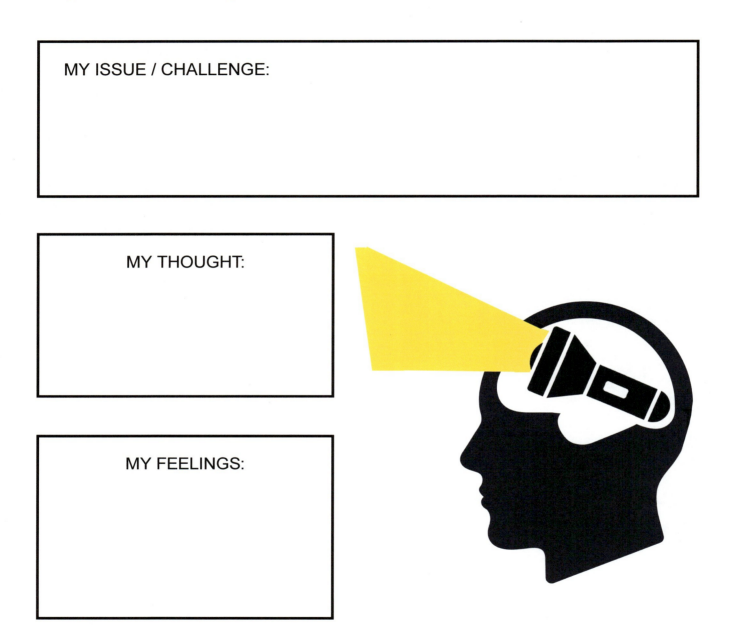

MY ISSUE / CHALLENGE:

MY THOUGHT:

MY FEELINGS:

OK. Now use your <mark>MIND FLASHLIGHT</mark> to shine onto **OTHER <u>NEW</u> THOUGHTS** that will help you **FEEL** the way **YOU WANT...**

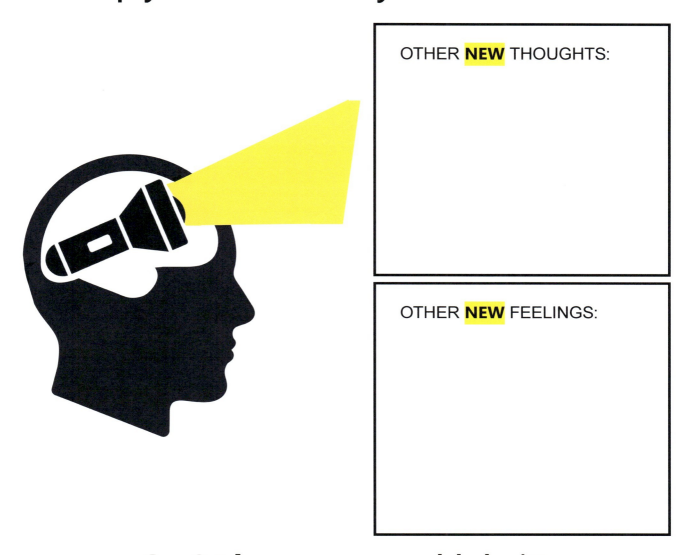

OTHER <mark>NEW</mark> THOUGHTS:

OTHER <mark>NEW</mark> FEELINGS:

See? I <u>knew</u> you could do it!

Here are some other blank sheets for you to use to help you practice using your

<mark>MIND FLASHLIGHT...</mark>

# MIND FLASHLIGHT PRACTICE SHEET

MY ISSUE / CHALLENGE:

MY THOUGHTS:

MY FEELINGS:

OR...

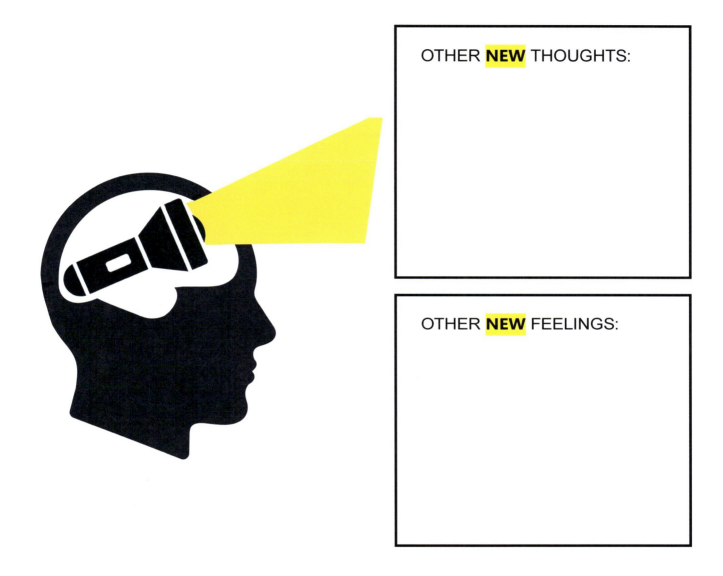

OTHER **NEW** THOUGHTS:

OTHER **NEW** FEELINGS:

# MIND FLASHLIGHT PRACTICE SHEET

MY ISSUE / CHALLENGE:

MY THOUGHTS:

MY FEELINGS:

OR...

OTHER **NEW** THOUGHTS:

OTHER **NEW** FEELINGS:

# MIND FLASHLIGHT PRACTICE SHEET

MY ISSUE / CHALLENGE:

MY THOUGHTS:

MY FEELINGS:

OR...

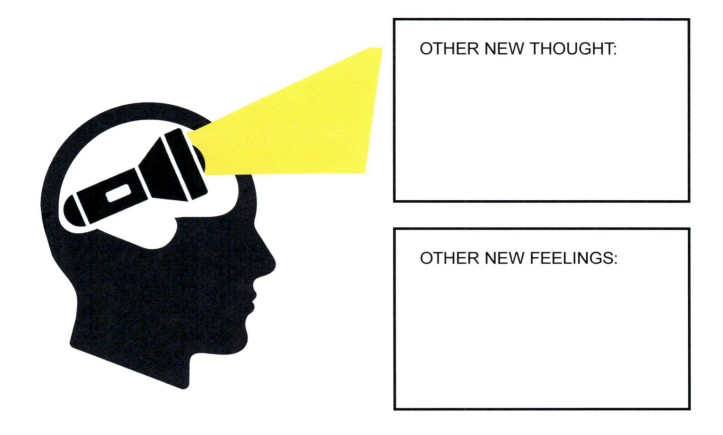

OTHER NEW THOUGHT:

OTHER NEW FEELINGS:

Additional copies of MIND FLASHLIGHT Practice Sheets can be downloaded for free at: www.theBOLDMoms.com

So, we NOW know...

You have this
**MIND FLASHLIGHT**.

You have **ULTIMATE CONTROL** of
your **MIND FLASHLIGHT**
(GREAT NEWS!)

You have **ULTIMATE CONTROL** what to
**light up** and what stays **IN. THE. DARK.**

**Light up the good?**

**Think good = feel good**

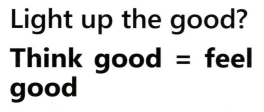

**Light up the bad?**

**Think bad = feel bad**

# YOUR CHOICE!

# I ASK YOU...

What do you want to shine your **MIND FLASHLIGHT** on?

Do you choose to shine it on
the **POSITIVE** or the **NEGATIVE**?

Do you choose to shine it on the
**POSSIBILITIES** or **IMPOSSIBILITIES**?

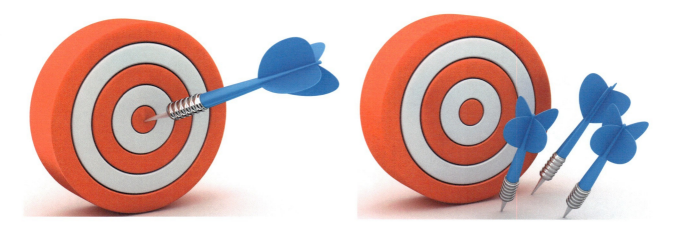

# Do you choose to shine it on

*the bummer
"woah is me - pity-party
for one" type of stuff*

*an empowered action
plan to make something
happen for yourself?*

## Or...

# Last Thoughts....

Our mind is designed to protect itself.
It does this by being on **ALERT!** and focusing on
the negative as a way to protect itself from what
it sees as dangerous territory.
Life does have it's bummer moments.
**Everyone's** life does.
And there will be times where it is totally acceptable and appropriate
to feel **MAD**, *sad*, **fRuStRaTeD**, (*insert any negative emotion here*).
In fact, everyone's life includes around 50% bummer moments.
**BUT....**

**YOU HAVE THE POWER** to put those
feelings in their appropriate place.

**YOU HAVE THE POWER** to take a
moment, *breathe*, and ask yourself:

*"Is it WORTH IT for me to THINK the bummer thoughts
and FEEL the bummer feelings for this situation?"*

If it <u>isn't worth it</u> to you and it <u>isn't serving you</u> to think those bummer thoughts and feel those bummer feelings, take your

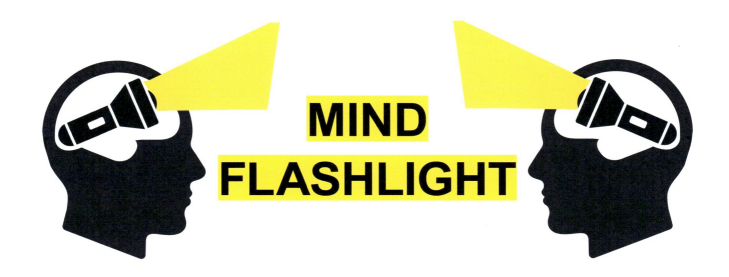

and shine it **SOMEWHERE ELSE**.

*It's all up to you. So....*

# KEEP
# CALM
## And
# SHINE
# ON

# About the Author:

*Stephanie Lambert* has been many things to many people, as most women and mothers are. Besides all the roles she plays as mom (referee, therapist, personal chef, gardener, tutor, housekeeper, chauffer...) she's been a high school teacher, a life coach, an amateur drummer, a professional dog walker, a blogger and is the founder of The BOLD Moms, a movement focused on encouraging moms (and their kids) to live their lives in BOLD. And now, we can add author to this list.

Stephanie lives in Redmond, Washington with her husband, her two sons and her chocolate German Shepherd, Lola.

She loves walking her dog, reading a good book, improving her drumming game, brunching with girlfriends and anytime spent at Diamond Lake in Eastern Washington with her family.